Construction Workers

Quinn M. Arnold

seedlings

CREATIVE EDUCATION • CREATIVE PAPERBACKS

Published by Creative Education and Creative Paperbacks
P.O. Box 227, Mankato, Minnesota 56002
Creative Education and Creative Paperbacks
are imprints of The Creative Company
www.thecreativecompany.us

Design by Ellen Huber; production by Christine Vanderbeek
Art direction by Rita Marshall
Printed in the United States of America

Photographs by Alamy (Folio Images, Jake Lyell),
Shutterstock (COOLKengzz, DutchScenery, Mike Flippo,
GIRODJL, goodluz, ifong, Dmitry Kalinovsky, Andreas G.
Karelias, Levent Konuk, kuponjabah, LifetimeStock, Menna,
michaeljung, Vladimir Nenezic, pbombaert, Csaba Peterdi,
Catalin Petolea, Photographee.eu, sculpies, vanchai)

Copyright © 2018 Creative Education, Creative Paperbacks
International copyright reserved in all countries. No part of
this book may be reproduced in any form without written
permission from the publisher.

Library of Congress Cataloging-in-Publication Data
Names: Arnold, Quinn M., author.
Title: Construction workers / Quinn M. Arnold.
Series: Seedlings.
Includes index.
Summary: A kindergarten-level introduction to construction
workers, covering their job description, the places where
they work, and how they help the community by using their
building skills.
Identifiers: LCCN 2016059792
ISBN 978-1-60818-871-0 (hardcover)
ISBN 978-1-62832-486-0 (pbk)
ISBN 978-1-56660-919-7 (eBook)
Subjects: LCSH: Construction workers—Juvenile literature.
Classification: LCC TH159.A76 2017 / DDC 338.7/624—dc23
CCSS: RI.K.1, 2, 3, 4, 5, 6, 7;
RI.1.1, 2, 3, 4, 5, 6, 7; RF.K.1, 3; RF.1.1

First Edition HC 9 8 7 6 5 4 3 2 1
First Edition PBK 9 8 7 6 5 4 3 2 1

TABLE OF CONTENTS

Hello, Construction Workers! 5

Community Builders 7

Construction Crews 8

Hard at Work 10

Tools of the Trade 12

On the Worksite 14

What Do Construction Workers Do? 17

Goodbye, Construction Workers! 18

Picture a Construction Worker 20

Words to Know 22

Read More 23

Websites 23

Index 24

Hello, construction workers!

Construction workers build schools, hospitals, and homes. They work on roads and bridges. They make parks.

A construction worker is part of a **crew**. Crews work outside and inside. Some even work at night.

A crew takes down an old building. Then workers build a new one.

Crews fix broken roads. They make new ones, too.

Strong construction workers use power tools on the job.

Some drive big trucks.

Construction workers want to stay safe. They wear hard hats and heavy boots. Many also wear bright vests.

Construction workers build and fix things. They work hard to make communities stronger.

Picture a Construction Worker

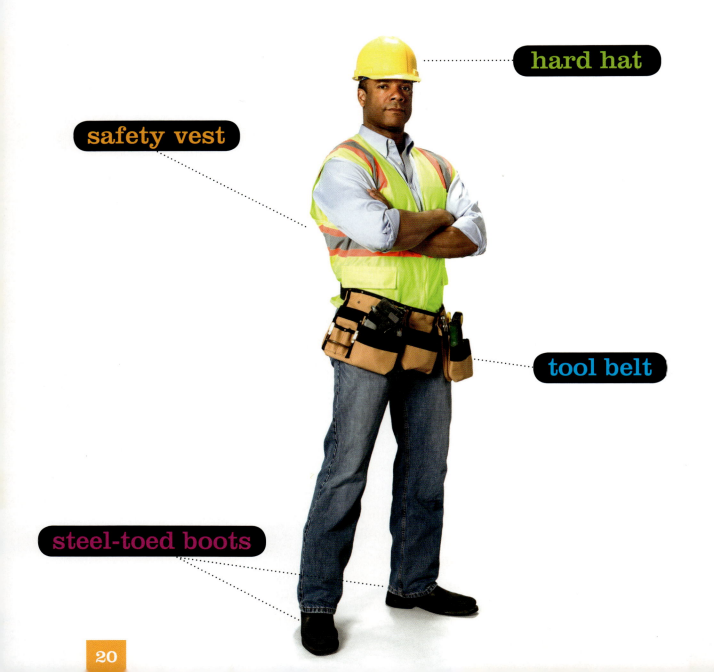

Words to Know

crew: a group of people who work together

hard hats: stiff, protective hats worn at construction sites

Read More

Hayden, Kate. *Amazing Buildings*. New York: DK, 2003.

Meister, Cari. *Construction Workers*. Minneapolis: Jump!, 2015.

Websites

PBS: Building Big
http://www.pbs.org/wgbh/buildingbig/abt_chall.html
Learn more about construction materials as you build different structures.

Science Kids: Engineering Facts
http://www.sciencekids.co.nz/sciencefacts/engineering/buildings.html
Learn construction facts about famous buildings.

Note: Every effort has been made to ensure that the websites listed above are suitable for children, that they have educational value, and that they contain no inappropriate materia . However, because of the nature of the Internet, it is impossible to guarantee that these sites will remain active indefinitely or that their contents will not be altered.

Index

boots 14

bridges 7

buildings 7, 10

crews 8, 10, 11

hard hats 14

parks 7

roads 7, 11

tools 12

vests 14